# KINGDOM BUILDERS

## HOW TO LIVE AN ALL IN LIFE THAT TURNS VISION INTO REALITY

### LAUNCH GUIDE
*Andrew Denton*

Kingdom Builders Launch Guide
Copyright © 2021 by Andrew Denton

All rights reserved. No part of this publication may be reproduced, stored in a retrieval system, or transmitted in any form by any means, electronic, mechanical, photocopy, recording, or otherwise, without the prior permission of the publisher, except as provided for by Australian copyright law.

Based on, and including excerpts from, *Kingdom Builders: How to live an ALL IN life that turns vision into reality* by Andrew Denton. Copyright © 2020 by Andrew Denton. Used by permission.

Scripture quotations marked MSG are taken from THE MESSAGE, copyright © 1993, 2002, 2018 by Eugene H. Peterson. Used by permission of NavPress. All rights reserved. Represented by Tyndale House Publishers, Inc.

Scripture quotations marked NIV are taken from THE HOLY BIBLE, NEW INTERNATIONAL VERSION®, NIV® Copyright © 1973, 1978, 1984, 2011 by Biblica, Inc.® Used by permission. All rights reserved worldwide.

First printing 2021
Cataloguing – in – Publication data available

ISBN 978-1-922411-29-7 (international trade paperback)
ISBN 978-1-922411-30-3 (ebook)

Cover & interior design: Felix Molonfalean
Cover photography: Tony Irving
Editor: Celina Mina

*God can do anything,
you know—far more than you could ever
imagine or guess or request
in your wildest dreams!*

Ephesians 3:20 MSG

# CONTENTS

| | |
|---|---|
| A Note from Andrew Denton | 9 |
| How To Use This Launch Pack | 11 |

**Introduction Session: For Pastors and Church Leaders**
    How to launch Kingdom Builders in your local church — 13

**Session 1: Exactly the Same Faith**
    An invitation to an "all in" life — 27

**Session 2: The Principles**
    Laying a Biblical foundation — 37

**Session 3: The Partners**
    Establishing intentional relationships — 51

**Session 4: The Practice**
    Building resilience and perseverance — 59

About the Author — 71

*A NOTE FROM*

## ANDREW DENTON

I am so excited that you have chosen to be a part of launching Kingdom Builders in your local church!

If you have never met me or heard me speak before, I'm a property development business owner and a long-time elder at Hillsong Church, based in Sydney, Australia. My beautiful wife, Susan, and I recently celebrated 36 years of marriage. We have three adult children who are also married, and three grandchildren.

Up until the COVID-19 pandemic hit us all in 2020, I traveled the world speaking in churches about raising finance for the Kingdom of God. Obviously, as a result of lockdowns and travel restrictions, this all changed! However, God used this for good: I prayerfully started thinking of scaleable ways to share the message of Kingdom Builders that would give me the ability to reach far more people than I could otherwise do in my lifetime.

The result was my first book, *Kingdom Builders: How to live an "all in" life that turns vision into reality*. When the book was released, so many pastors and church leaders reached out to me, asking questions about how to practically launch Kingdom Builders in their own church. In addition, many people from different churches told me that as a result of reading my book, they really felt called to be a Kingdom Builder but were planted in a church without a Kingdom Builders ministry.

This caused my team and I to create the Kingdom Builders Launch Pack.

As you watch the teaching videos, complete the workbook components, and actively participate in discussions with your group, it is my prayer that you will gain the wisdom and practical tools needed to live the life of a Kingdom Builder and witness the vision of your local church turn into reality.

*HOW TO*

---

## USE THIS LAUNCH PACK

The Kingdom Builders Launch Pack includes:

- The Launch Guide
- The Study Guide
- Accompanying teaching videos for each session

The Launch Guide is specifically for pastors and church leaders. We encourage you to complete the sessions in this guide together as a leadership team. You can work through it at your own pace based on a time frame that suits your team the best. You might decide to complete one session per week over five weeks, or to go through all the sessions as part of an intensive planning day or leadership retreat.

The Launch Guide contains an additional introductory session and accompanying teaching video, which aims to unpack the practical steps involved in launching Kingdom Builders in your local church. After completing the introduction, you will go on and complete sessions 1-4 as a leadership team. Once you have completed all the sessions, you will be able to facilitate sessions 1-4 with those from your congregation who self-identify as Kingdom Builders. Again, the time frame and setting is up to each church to decide and plan. Participants will need to refer to the original book, *Kingdom Builders: How to live an "all in" life that turns vision into reality*, and have a copy of or access to the church vision statement.

The Study Guide is specifically for church congregation members. Each session begins with a teaching video by Andrew Denton. Teaching Notes for each video are provided with space for participants to make their own notes. Following the teaching, participants are then invited to complete the Application questions. A Personal Notes section is provided for participants to write down any further reflections and ideas. To conclude, participants are encouraged to discuss some of their answers in pairs or small groups.

After the first session, we recommend setting time at the beginning of the second session for participants to share further reflections they have had between sessions. This sharing time can also take place at the start of sessions 3 and 4.

*INTRODUCTION SESSION:*

---

# FOR PASTORS AND CHURCH LEADERS

*How to launch Kingdom Builders in your local church*

**Teaching Notes:**

As you watch the teaching video for this session, use the following outline to record anything that stands out to you:

The role of "Kings" and "Priests" in the church.

.................................................................................

.................................................................................

.................................................................................

The pastors set the vision, but the Kingdom Builders set the pace.

It is about equal sacrifice, not equal giving.

Every church must have a vision that is communicated clearly to the entire congregation.

*The Kingdom Builders of our own church have made significant personal sacrifices in order that the vision and mission of our church can take leaps and bounds forward and I don't know where we would be without them. They stretch and extend themselves. They believe that their lives can play a significant part in building the very thing that God Himself says He is building—His Church. The fruit of the weekly salvations we see at Hillsong Church is their fruit also—borne from a heart to make Hillsong—their place of planting—a HOME for others.*

*I believe that every pastor needs a core group of men and women just like this. People who love the House of God. People who are committed to leaning into the vision of their planting, to trusting and supporting leadership, and to Godly stewardship of what they themselves have been given.*

*The Body of Christ is full of innovative men and women making a difference who recognize that Kingdom Builders are church builders; they recognize their lives are about more than themselves; they are men and women who have a revelation of the PURPOSE and CAUSE for which they are living.*

— **Excerpt from the Foreword by Brian Houston**
*Kingdom Builders: How to live an "all in" life that turns vision into reality*

## *CHECKLIST*

☐ Does the pastor have a clear vision for the church?

☐ Have you identified one Kingdom Builder to share their testimony?

☐ Have you set a date for the launch to your whole church?

☐ Have you adequately promoted the event to your congregation?

☐ Have you created Kingdom Builder application forms for people to write out their pledges? These can be printed and/or made available online. The application form should contain the following fields:

> *• First and last name*
> *• Email address/phone number*
> *• Business name and business ID number (if giving through their business)*
> *• Pledge amount (what they plan to give that year above their usual tithes)*
> *• Name of their connect group leader/team leader/ service pastor etc. (these people can be contacted if there are any pastoral care concerns about the applicant)*

- ☐ Have you worked out the minimum amount to give to be a Kingdom Builder? This amount will differ based on the economy and context of your location.

- ☐ Have your provided the different methods and banking details needed for Kingdom Builders to transfer their giving?

- ☐ Have you set aside 30-minute time slots for one-on-one conversations?

- ☐ Do you have adequate stock of the book, *Kingdom Builders: How to live an "all in" life that turns vision into reality* to give to those who self-identify as Kingdom Builders?

- ☐ Have you planned and scheduled the Kingdom Builders Study Guide sessions 1-4?

- ☐ Have you scheduled other Kingdom Builder events in the church calendar to honor and invest in your Kingdom Builders?

## *ONE-ON-ONE QUESTIONS:*

• What resonated with you the most from the Kingdom Builders presentation?

• Do you read your Bible daily with expectation?

• Do you pray daily with your spouse?

• If you're single, do you have two other Godly people to pray with daily?

• Do you have written goals and dreams for your life?

• Are you on the same page spiritually with your spouse/fiancé? (If married/engaged)

• What is holding you back from going "all-in" with God?

• Are you living a fearful or faithful life? Why?

• What are you believing God for as a result of this simple invitation?

*AN OPEN LETTER*

———

## TO PASTORS EVERYWHERE

Dear Pastor,

Your church is waiting for you to do the soul-searching, life-giving, earth-shaking work you've been called to.

They are eager to get behind your God-sized vision to advance the Kingdom beyond what even you can ask for, think or imagine.

A handful are desperately anticipating and praying for the opportunity to be stretched, challenged, mobilized, and called out to give, go, pray, and lead.

Yes. Their eyes are glued on you. They are watching to see if you are who you say you are. And, that you'll do what God has called you to do. They want to know if you are for real. They want to see what you'll do first. If you will...

Serve first.
Give first.
Dream first.
Pray first.

Go first.

And, they truly believe and want to go "all-in". They really do.

But, they're waiting.

Yes. They're waiting to be challenged by a God-sized vision that calls out the best in who they are and what they believe is possible. They are waiting to be called to life out on the edge. Kingdom life.

The life they've read about in the Scriptures.

The life you preach about week in and week out.

The abundant life God promises over and over in the Scriptures.

But they need you to paint a picture of where God is calling your church to.

What your vision for them as a community of sold-out, "all-in" believers really looks like. The big-hairy-audacious-vision that scares you.

You know. The one you surrendered your life and calling to be a part of. That God-sized vision that is beyond your wildest dreams and aspirations. The one that requires God to show up and show off. The vision that you've been to afraid to speak out loud.

Your playing small doesn't do anyone any good. Especially your church family. Your inability to dream big is causing them to play small, too. They are tiptoeing around the truth, because you are.

Don't let your ego get in the way.

Don't let your lack of faith paralyze you.

Don't let anything big or small stop you.

Do whatever it is that you need to do to hear from God. To dream with Him. To see the potential that He sees. To capture the hearts of the people He's entrusted to your care.

Don't shrink back.

Don't play small.

Don't waste another Sunday. Another sermon. Another moment.

Get on your knees. Open up your heart. And, ask for the impossible.

Then take what God speaks to you back to your people. Speak that vision into reality. Call out the best in them. And, invite them to join you in making that God-sized dream a reality.

Your people are waiting.

God is waiting.

And, deep down you're waiting.

Now is the time.

Stop procrastinating and start believing.

You have been called to so much more. To build the Kingdom. And, to raise up Kingdom Builders.

Sincerely,

Andrew & Susan Denton

— Excerpt from *Kingdom Builders: How to live an "all in" life that turns vision into reality*

## *APPLICATION:*

1. Review any notes that you wrote down while viewing the teaching video for this session. Share one thing that stood out to you the most with your group.

2. As a leadership team, read through the vision of your church and discuss how effectively it is currently being communicated to your congregation.

3. Use the provided Checklist and One-on-One Questions for the 30-minute meetings to plan how your church is going to launch Kingdom Builders across your Sunday services.

**Personal Notes:**

**Personal Notes:**

**Personal Notes:**

SESSION 1:

---

# EXACTLY THE SAME FAITH

*An invitation to an "all in" life*

**Teaching Notes:**

As you watch the teaching video for this session, use the following outline to record anything that stands out to you:

There is a difference between "being IN" and "being ALL IN".

....................................................................................................

....................................................................................................

....................................................................................................

"But seek FIRST his Kingdom and his righteousness, and all these things will be given to you as well." Matthew 6:33 NIV (emphasis added).

Everyone wants the ALL; not everyone wants to SURRENDER ALL to God.

"God can do anything, you know—far more than you could ever imagine or guess or request in your wildest dreams!" Ephesians 3:20 MSG

## Fear vs. Faith

## Taking steps of faith.

## *APPLICATION:*

1. Review any notes that you wrote down while viewing the teaching video for this session. Share one thing that stood out to you the most with your group.

2. Reflect on your life thus far. Make lists of significant milestones and events, the education and qualifications you have received and/or are currently completing, and the different jobs and career paths you have had and/or are currently in. What patterns emerge as you read over these lists? How has God been at work in your life using all these things together for good?

3. Write down all your talents and skills (not just those connected to your formal training and employment), your passions, and any ways that you currently serve in your local church.

........................................................................................................

........................................................................................................

........................................................................................................

........................................................................................................

........................................................................................................

........................................................................................................

........................................................................................................

........................................................................................................

4. Read through your church vision statement. What parts inspire you and cause excitement?

........................................................................................................

........................................................................................................

........................................................................................................

5. Conclude your personal notes by writing a Faith Declaration to God in the form of a prayer. In your own words, express your desire to live an "all in" life, and ask for wisdom, strength and courage to surrender all things to God and take steps of faith.

..................................................................................................

..................................................................................................

..................................................................................................

..................................................................................................

..................................................................................................

..................................................................................................

6. What is the next faith step that you are going to take in relation to fulfilling your purpose as a Kingdom Builder?

..................................................................................................

..................................................................................................

..................................................................................................

**Personal Notes:**

**Personal Notes:**

## Personal Notes:

*SESSION 2:*

# THE PRINCIPLES

*Laying a Biblical foundation*

**Teaching Notes:**

As you watch the teaching video for this session, use the following outline to record anything that stands out to you:

Principle 1: Tithing

........................................................................................................

........................................................................................................

........................................................................................................

We don't give our tithe; we bring our tithe.

"Bring the whole tithe into the storehouse, that there may be food in my house. Test me in this," says the Lord Almighty, "and see if I will not throw open the floodgates of heaven and pour out so much blessing that there will not be room enough to store it." - Malachi 3:10 NIV

Principle 2: Stewardship

## The Parable of the Talents (Matthew 25:14-30)

## Faith is spelled R-I-S-K

## Principle 3: Sowing and Reaping

"Do not be deceived: God cannot be mocked. A man reaps what he sows. Whoever sows to please their flesh, from the flesh will reap destruction; whoever sows to please the Spirit, from the Spirit will reap eternal life." - Galatians 6:7-8 NIV

Business mission statement.

Principle 4: Obedience

## The story of the rich young ruler (Mark 10)

## Principle 5: Generosity

## Money magnifies who you really are.

"The world of the generous gets larger and larger; the world of the stingy gets smaller and smaller." - Proverbs 11:24 MSG

If God can get it THROUGH you, He will get it TO you.

## *APPLICATION:*

1. Review any notes that you wrote down while viewing the teaching video for this session. Share one thing that stood out to you the most with your group.

2. What is your current view on tithing? What has shaped your view on tithing? How does your view compare with the Bible passages and teaching shared in this session?

_____

_____

_____

_____

_____

_____

3. Out of the five principles, which ones are you actively applying in your own life? Are there any that you need to start applying? What is one way you can begin applying that principle this week?

4. In the book, *Kingdom Builders*, there is a chapter called "The Ministry of What?" Andrew Denton writes that his ministry is to finance the Kingdom. In your own words, describe what your ministry is.

5. Throughout his book, Andrew Denton states that being a Kingdom Builder is not about the money; it's a heart condition. What does this mean to you?

6. "Denton's Four D's" stand for daily, deliberate, disciplined decisions. What daily decisions have you made or need to make in different areas of your life? List them on the next page:

| AREA | DAILY DECISION |
|---|---|
| Relationship with God | |
| Marriage | |
| Family | |
| Physical health | |
| Mental/Emotional health | |
| Fellowship | |
| Finances | |
| Work | |
| Personal development | |
| Other | |

## Personal Notes:

**Personal Notes:**

**Personal Notes:**

*SESSION 3:*

---

# THE PARTNERS

*Establishing intentional relationships*

**Teaching Notes:**

As you watch the teaching video for this session, use the following outline to record anything that stands out to you:

Partner 1: The Holy Spirit

......................................................................................................................

......................................................................................................................

......................................................................................................................

Are you praying everyday for God to guide your path?
Are you asking for unfair advantage?
Are you asking for the wealth of the wicked for your righteous plans?

............................................................................................................................

............................................................................................................................

............................................................................................................................

Partner 2: Your Spouse (if married) or A Prayer Group

............................................................................................................................

............................................................................................................................

............................................................................................................................

Praying together daily.

............................................................................................................................

............................................................................................................................

............................................................................................................................

30 days, 4 months, 1 year

Partner 3: The Next Generation

Partner 4: Your Pastor and Church Leaders

Partner 5: A Network

## *APPLICATION:*

1. Review any notes that you wrote down while viewing the teaching video for this session. Share one thing that stood out to you the most with your group.

2. It is important to take stock and complete a Relationship Inventory. Reflect on the different types of partnerships explored in this session: the Holy Spirit, your spouse, a prayer group, the next generation, your pastor and church leaders, and a network. List specific names of people who make up those partnerships in your life and next to their name, write down what role they have in your life.

3. Are there any partnerships that you need to intentionally establish or strengthen? How will you do that?

4. What roles do you play in the lives of others?

**Personal Notes:**

**Personal Notes:**

*SESSION 4:*

---

# THE PRACTICE

*Building resilience and perseverance*

**Teaching Notes:**

As you watch the teaching video for this session, use the following outline to record anything that stands out to you:

Living by faith.

...........................................................................................................................

...........................................................................................................................

...........................................................................................................................

There's no such thing as a wrong step.

"The Lord makes firm the steps of the one who delights in him; though he may stumble, he will not fall, for the Lord upholds him with his hand." - Psalm 37:23-24 NIV

Take a wise step (due diligence).

"Under attack means I'm right on track."

"The thief comes only to steal and kill and destroy; I have come that they may have life, and have it to the full." - John 10:10 NIV

"Be alert and of sober mind. Your enemy the devil prowls around LIKE a roaring lion looking for someone to devour." - 1 Peter 5:8 NIV (emphasis added)

Put on the full armor of God (Ephesians 6).

In the midst of uncertainty, we need to build upon God's certain promises.

Opportunity comes to those who are prepared.

I'm ALL IN for God.
I'm a Kingdom Builder.
I believe in the vision of my church.
I've got my pastor's back.

## *APPLICATION:*

1. Review any notes that you wrote down while viewing the teaching video for this session. Share one thing that stood out to you the most with your group.

2. As Kingdom Builders, we are called to be faithful, not fearful. Not just in finances but in every area of life. Think about your current season and set of circumstances. Are there any faith steps that you are holding back from taking? Why? Write down what those faith steps are and what you are specifically worried about.

3. Read over your response to the previous question. How does the statement, "There's no such thing as a wrong step," apply to this situation?

4. Reflect on the tough times that you have had to navigate in the past. What have times of crisis and challenge taught you?

5. Do you read your Bible daily? If you do, write down the main theme that is currently coming up in your Bible reading time. How does it connect with the timing of this study? If you don't, download a one-year Bible reading plan from YouVersion and begin today!

....................................................................................................

....................................................................................................

....................................................................................................

....................................................................................................

....................................................................................................

....................................................................................................

6. Write down the names of two people to whom you are going to send your "verse of the day".

....................................................................................................

....................................................................................................

....................................................................................................

7. Have you written down your dreams and goals for the next month, year, and five years? If you have, do you read them daily? Are they big audacious goals or small easily-achieved goals? If you haven't written them down, make time this week to set aside time to prayerfully write down those dreams and goals.

**Personal Notes:**

**Personal Notes:**

*ABOUT*

## THE AUTHOR

Andrew Denton is a successful business owner and long-time elder at Hillsong Church who has circled the globe sharing a simple message: inspiring pastors and their congregations to live life on a different level and finance the Kingdom. He's also raised three wonderful, God-fearing children alongside his beautiful bride, Susan. As a kid he wanted to be a professional surfer and travel the world; God answered one of those prayers. When Andrew's not surfing, texting Denton's Daily Verse out to leaders around the planet, or drinking a long-black, you can find him enjoying time with his grandkids at home in Sydney, Australia. Relational, honest and straight-forward, Andrew's approach to ministry and life is nothing short of inspirational. His talks have impacted thousands of believers world-wide. Which is why the truths found within these pages will challenge you to become a Kingdom Builder and change the way you serve God forever.

**Kingdom Builders: How to live an "all-in" life that turns vision into reality**

Living a life of generosity is not reserved for rich people. It's the result of people who are "all in" for giving God permission to use them as a conduit of His blessing and provision.

Kingdom Builders know that they are alive for a purpose bigger than themselves—a purpose committed to building His Kingdom and turning church vision into a magnificent global and local reality.

Sharing from his own journey of living an "all in" life, and telling the inspiring story of how Kingdom Builders first started within Hillsong Church, Andrew Denton will encourage and challenge you to take bold, wise steps of faith that will lead you on a path beyond your wildest dreams.

Get your copy at kingdombuildersbook.com

**Check out other resources by Andrew Denton at kingdombuildersbook.com**

- The Kingdom Builders Podcast
- The Kingdom Builders 7-day YouVersion Devotional

## Personal Notes:

**Personal Notes:**

**Personal Notes:**

**Personal Notes:**

## Personal Notes:

www.ingramcontent.com/pod-product-compliance
Lightning Source LLC
Chambersburg PA
CBHW071122160426
43196CB00013B/2671